THE **INSIDERS** GUIDE

Choosing a secondary school and GETTING in

This is how it works. Make it work for you.

Ange Tyler and Liz Lewis

GW00720742

Published by Capital Talent
Copyright © 2010 Capital Talent UK
All Rights Reserved

Us

We have been advising friends and family about their school choices for years. We have lived with their anxieties and disappointments and often been consulted too late. At a social event recently, an acquaintance deciding where best to buy a house was shocked to find that her assumptions about the quality of schools in two of her nearby Local Authorities were the reverse of their actual performance.

We have worked as successful school leaders in international, independent and highly selective grammar schools and as part of recovery teams in badly failing rural and inner city schools. We have seen and operated the system from all sides and we are passionate about making it better and fairer. From years of success in Headship and school improvement we know there is much more to a good school than examination results: as parents and carers, you need to know that your child will be able to make the most of their abilities, academically and personally.

We have written this guide because we want you to know what we know and see what we see when we look at a good school.

We have written this guide to put within your grasp a good school for your child, a school where your expectations are raised, your child's aspirations met, and potential realised.

You

The time of every child automatically transferring to a local secondary school is well and truly gone. Yet despite all the talk about parent choice, of the half a million families who apply for secondary school places each year, tens of thousands are denied their top three choices and many thousands are given places at a school they didn't choose at all.

So what can you do? We believe that with the best information available you can maximise your choices. Knowing how to interpret that information and knowing how the Local Authority and schools operate within the system can only strengthen your hand.

FOLLOWING THE GUIDE

Our experience tells us that the following things are key to choosing and getting your child into the right Secondary School:

- Separating your **available** and **unavailable** choices

- Avoiding the mistakes others have made when applying

- Deciding what's right for your child (and your family)

- Collecting information from schools and understanding what it tells you

- Visiting schools and interpreting what you see and hear

- Comparing the schools you like, remembering that they will be very different in:

    how they look, are organised and run

    their cultures and values

    their curriculum offer, pathways to careers and further study, opportunities outside the classroom and particular strengths

    the relationships they build with you as parents and carers.

Each section in the Guide covers one or more of these key elements and gives you questions to think about and answer.

1. ADMISSIONS

2. YOU AND YOUR CHILD

3. INFORMATION FROM THE SCHOOL

4. INFORMATION ABOUT THE SCHOOL

5. THE VISIT

6. PLAYING YOUR PART

This is not a test.
There are no right or wrong answers.

The Guide is a framework to support your information gathering, understanding and decision making not a straight jacket to suffocate your common sense, judgement or preferences.

TO MAKE THE MOST
OF EACH SECTION:

Read the whole Guide. You can do this in any order. We know that some of you will want to read it out of sequence or to dip in and out, so each section makes sense on its own.

Use the questions in each section for each school you are considering and record your answers so that you can make properly informed comparisons.

Add to your answers once you have made your school visits.

Once you have finished all the questions in the guide you will have collected enough information to fill in the separate comparison chart. This will summarise the main points to inform your final decision.

Take the Guide with you on your school visits to remind you what to look for.

Go to our website at www.capitaltalent.co.uk and click on Getting In for additional information and ideas where you see the arrow.

Then choose the information you wish to see. The phrase you need to look for on the web page is in **bold type**.

Ask yourself why a school has made the decisions it has. Are decisions made to suit the needs of the students, to provide them with wider opportunities or to organise the school to suit the adults? Often the same decisions are made for these two very different reasons and make for different communities and opportunities.

1.

ADMISSIONS

1. ADMISSIONS

This is the first place where you can increase your chances of success. To maximise these chances you need to understand:

THE ADMISSIONS PROCESS

HOW TO IDENTIFY YOUR AVAILABLE CHOICES

WHAT HAPPENS IF THERE ARE MORE APPLICATIONS THAN PLACES IN THE SCHOOLS YOU LIKE

HOW TO APPEAL

THE ADMISSIONS PROCESS

The admissions process operates nationally within the same timeframe and guidelines. It is co-ordinated locally by every Council or Authority on behalf of all state schools. The rules are laid out in the School Admissions Code, a long and complex document which every school and Local Authority must abide by.

 www.capitaltalent.co.uk to see a copy of the **School Admissions Code**.

The exact dates for each Local Authority are slightly different but fall within:

When	What
May of Year 5 in primary school.	Local Authorities publish details of where you can see admissions details for the following September.
September/October of Year 6.	Local Authorities send you a list of your local schools and an explanation of the process (often via primary schools).
September/October of Year 6.	School open evenings and open days (visits).
October/November of Year 6.	Completion and return of your application to Local Authority.
March 1st of Year 6.	Letter or email informing you of your offer (including information on how to appeal).
March/April Year 6.	Appeals made and heard.

 www.capitaltalent.co.uk for information on **how to apply if you arrive in an area after March**.

Important to remember:

All dates vary slightly so check carefully.

The number of choices you will be given varies between 3 and 6, depending on your Local Authority.

Every state school is included in the process so you must make all your choices through the Local Authority even if some of your schools also require a separate application form.

If you do apply to a school that requires you to complete a separate application form, **check the closing date**, as it may be different from the Local Authority's deadline.

If you miss the deadline, your application will be considered **after** those that arrived on time.

HOW TO IDENTIFY YOUR AVAILABLE CHOICES

You need to be clear about every state school in your area.

In September of your child's Year 6 of primary school, **your Local Authority or Council will send you their list**.

But you may also wish to request the lists from other Local Authorities to broaden your options.

Next you need to separate your available from your unavailable choices. To do this you need to collect and read the admissions criteria for each school you like.

Whoever makes and operates the rules for admissions to a school is known as the Admissions Authority.

The Admission Authority for each school you are considering will either be:

The Local Authority

Or

The school itself.

This depends on the official status or type of school (You can get this information from the school or the Local Authority).

Once you know what type of school each is you will know where to get the admissions criteria and who will operate them.

Most schools put their admissions criteria on the Local Authority web site.

The table below shows you which Admissions Authority belongs with which type of school.

Type of school	Admissions Authority
Community	Local Authority
Foundation (and Trust)	School (Governing Body)
Voluntary Aided	School (Governing Body)
Voluntary Controlled	Local Authority
Academies	School (Governing Body)

 These are the most common. Go to **www.capitaltalent.co.uk** to see the **full range of state schools**.

You will also need to identify which schools on the list operate a selection test like the 11+. Decide whether you think your child has a realistic chance of passing. Your primary school will be able to give you the best advice on this.

www.capitaltalent.co.uk for **guidance on preparing for entrance exams**.

Important to remember:

Read the criteria carefully. Schools and Local Authorities are allowed to change them every year so don't go on hearsay from last year.

Read them all: just because you don't fit one of the criteria doesn't mean you won't qualify for a place.

Don't make assumptions about what will be included in the criteria: there are plenty of Church of England schools or Academies who take a percentage of pupils from their local communities regardless of faith or ability.

Don't trust acquaintances with whom you are in competition for places – they might try to mislead you!

Medical grounds give your child priority in many cases, and children in care or fostered should always get priority.

Some schools with religious sounding names are community or voluntary controlled and are not actually Faith schools. **Check**.

If you do apply to a school where you don't fulfil the criteria, you will not be considered but your application will count as one of your choices. **Avoid this expensive mistake**.

Local authority admissions authorities

Local Authority schools tend to serve a locality except for grammar schools which take from a wider area. They usually give places to:

- Children who live within a certain distance of the school

- Children who already have brothers and sisters at the school

However, if more children live in the area than there are places within the school then other considerations come into play. The oversubscription criteria will explain what happens in this situation.

 www.capitaltalent.co.uk if you want advice on **applying outside the Local Authority where you live**.

Schools as admissions authorities

Even if a school decides its own criteria for admission, it is still bound by the rules of the School Admissions Code.

Some of the main rules are summarised here:

Schools MUST NOT	Schools MUST
use interviews, tests (except for grammar schools and specialist schools partially selecting for aptitude) or photographs to select pupils.	publish the number of 11 year olds they will admit and stick to that number.
ask to meet parents by any means as part of the selection process for example say that you must attend an Open Evening or collect or return an application in person.	meet all the requirements of equalities legislation.
ask for money in the form of voluntary contributions or practical help as volunteers as part of the admissions process.	apply their published criteria fairly and openly.
refuse an application from a pupil with a statement of special needs whose parents have named that school.	tell you why you didn't get a place and explain how you can appeal.

www.capitaltalent.co.uk if the admissions authority operates
a system called **random allocation**.

School specialisms

Most schools in England now have a specialism to develop Centres
of Curriculum Excellence in one or two areas. They are a vehicle for
school improvement and act as a key lever to raise standards across
the whole school and to share expertise with others.

- These schools are supported by Government funding to establish
  a distinctive identity and excellence using the specialisms.

- The funding supports curriculum development in specialist
  areas and provides networking at local, regional, national and
  international levels.

- It is important to find out what specialisms are held by the
  schools you are considering, and ask whether any of them match
  your own child's strengths or interests.

- These schools can use their specialisms to admit 10% of their
  pupils based on talent or aptitude in that subject area (where
  they have two Specialisms, 20%).

- Schools **do not have** to use the specialism to select. Many do not
  operate selection of any kind.

- The opportunities afforded your child, if they are accepted under
  the terms of the specialism, can be exciting and unique.

 www.capitaltalent.co.uk to see **current areas of specialism**.

WHAT HAPPENS IF THERE ARE MORE APPLICATIONS THAN PLACES IN THE SCHOOL I LIKE?

When a school or Local Authority receives more eligible applications than it has places, it uses its over-subscription criteria to award places .

Admissions authorities must publish these criteria. (Examples of appropriate tie-breakers are clearly set down in the Code)

Where schools are traditionally popular, look at their oversubscription criteria along with the rest of their admissions criteria. If you are clearly eligible to apply then these will tell you how likely it is you will be awarded a place.

These criteria will be central to your case if you are going to appeal against a decision.

Here is a summary of the main guidance from the Code:

Admissions authorities must not:	Admissions authorities can prioritise:
make unreasonable stipulations.	siblings of children who are still at the school.
operate 'first preference first'.	siblings at primary schools.
favour those whose parents have offered help or money, children of staff members or governors.	siblings at secondary schools.

use reports from previous schools.	social and medical need.
discriminate against children with SEN or disabilities.	a designated catchment area.
favour relatives of former pupils or siblings who have left.	ease of access by transport.
favour or discriminate in any other way.	distance between home and school.
take parents' marital, financial or occupational status into account.	the ethos of the school (schools can ask all parents applying for a place to respect the ethos and its importance to the school community, but such statements must be factual).
	specific feeder primary schools (having named feeder schools must not unfairly disadvantage children from more deprived areas near the school and **must not** include independent schools as named feeder schools).
	pupil ability banding (to ensure that their intake includes a proportionate spread of children of different abilities. It can apply to a single school, a group - such as a Federation- or the whole LA).

HOW TO APPEAL

Like the admissions process, the appeals process has specific guidelines which must be followed.

 www.capitaltalent.co.uk for a full explanation of **how to appeal**.

Important to remember:

These are some of the main pitfalls. Of course many boil down to that old teacher's advice **'read the instructions carefully.'**

Check dates and deadlines and follow them. By law the Admissions Authorities have to stick strictly to them.

Be aware that if you put a popular school second or third on your list, you are unlikely to get it as one of your choices. It will fill up with first choice places. This means that if you don't get your first choice you will probably be offered a place not on your list at all.

If you are applying to a school that requires a separate application form you MUST still name this school on your Local Authority form and RETURN it to the Local Authority. ONLY schools on your Local Authority application will be considered as your choices.

Take all your choices seriously and don't assume you will get your first choice. In some parts of the country only 50% of parents and carers get their first choices. Your second and third choices need to be fully researched.

Make sure your application arrives on time. It's the arrival date that is considered the deadline not when you sent it.

Ask the school or the Local Authority, if you don't understand. There will be plenty of others who don't understand and they will be asking.

 www.capitaltalent.co.uk for **admissions FAQs**.

Which schools are we interested in?

School 1

School 2

School 3

School 4

School 5

School 6

Which criteria for each of these schools does my child meet?

School 1

School 2

School 3

School 4

School 5

School 6

Which further questions do I need to ask about the criteria for each school?

School 1

School 2

School 3

School 4

School 5

School 6

Do I need to complete a separate school application form?

School	Yes	No
School 1		
School 2		
School 3		
School 4		
School 5		
School 6		

2.

YOU AND
YOUR CHILD

2. YOU AND YOUR CHILD

In this section think about:

HOW YOU APPROACH YOUR CHOICES

YOUR CHILD AS A LEARNER

HOW YOU APPROACH YOUR CHOICES

Use these pointers when doing your homework on the schools, during the visits and finally when making your choices.

- A good school is not the same as a good school for your child.

You are looking for a match between what you and your child want from secondary education and what a given school has to offer. To get the right match you need to have thought about your child's strengths and needs and your family's values.

- You are looking for a school place for your child, not your friends' children.

And just because children get along doesn't mean that they need the same from school and friendship doesn't mean that you and your friends want the same for your children.

- Be aware of how schools have changed since you were a pupil: new subjects; different layout; all kinds of modern equipment and resources; Information Technology and interactive white boards, CAD cams, recording and television studios. You will certainly not recognise all the professionals working in or based in schools: resident artists, teaching assistants, mentors, youth workers, medics, social workers.

- Don't make your choices based on what friends and acquaintances say.

It's common for all of us to defend our decisions by hearing and repeating the good things about our choices and the bad things about options we rejected. Far better to ask questions of the children at the schools you are considering. They often can't help but tell the truth.

- Where do you see your child in 10 years?

Each school offers different pathways to further study or the world of work. Each has different strengths and different successes. Of course for an 11 year old the future is not set in stone but having some idea about direction will tell you whether this school is a match for you.

If you are not sure, go for a school with a range of pathways: A levels (or equivalent) for university and apprenticeships and vocational qualifications which combine study and preparation for the job market.

- Be clear about your family's values.

Your child will be in school many hours a week. You don't want your child to be in conflict at school or bringing home behaviours or attitudes you can't subscribe to.

- You are going to have worries.

'How will my child cope with the travelling?' 'Will s/he be bullied?' 'Will s/he make new friends?' 'Will I still be able to help with homework?' You are not alone in these anxieties and they are perfectly natural thoughts to have during this time of transition.

 www.capitaltalent.co.uk for more advice on **coping with worries**.

And once you start to visit....

- Don't get too absorbed in your own memories.

Actually going into a school building may well take you back. Whether secondary school was a positive and successful experience for you or whether you did not get what you needed from it, the familiar smells and sights may knock you off balance. Either way, don't get distracted from your purpose.

Important to remember:

Finally, you have to be the decision-maker.

There are things your child may want, things that you know are for the best and attractions that each school uses to promote itself. In amongst all of these you have to make a decision. While you will want to consult your child, it's right that you make the final choices.

YOUR CHILD AS A LEARNER

- Think about how your child prefers to learn.

You know that your child is unique but you may not have given a lot of thought to how s/he learns or realised yourself that there are several ways of learning.

- Understand preferred learning styles.

Are you reading this guide start to finish or did you go to some other section first, for example, The Visit? Are you interested by the graphics and colours or frankly, haven't you noticed? Your answers to these questions will partly be to do with how you take in information.

In summary, we all prefer one of three ways to learn:

- **Looking** - **Visual**

- **Listening** - **Auditory**

- **Moving** – **Kinaesthetic**

www.capitaltalent.co.uk for more information on **learning styles** including questionnaires you can use with your child.

- Compare how well each school uses learning styles.

Good schools will consciously give students practice in all three so that they become more competent all round learners and so that those who need to work quietly have as much chance to progress as those who need to talk or move to process information.

- Beware of schools who think children should be seen and not heard.

It is true to say that in some schools the predominant teaching style suits the child who likes to listen. This is not the way most children learn. Evidence shows that listening is not the domain of a particular ability either so don't be lured into thinking 'oh, my child is bright, s/he can learn anywhere.'

In the section on The Visit we show you what to look for and what to ask when you go around schools.

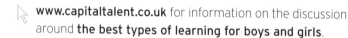 **www.capitaltalent.co.uk** for information on the discussion around **the best types of learning for boys and girls**.

Like all complex issues, some have tried to reduce it to simplistic explanations that are often misleading. What can be said is that what makes most difference to a child's long-term happiness and success is the learning habits they develop. These can be acquired regardless of gender.

- Think about how much your child depends on good relationships to learn.

Some children are very emotionally independent as learners. They will look to their peers for support and companionship or even use their own inner resources.

Others need a strong relationship with their teacher to progress.

When you look at relationships on your visit, bear this in mind. (More under The Visit.)

Which 3 things are the most important for me in choosing a secondary school?

1

2

3

Which 3 things are the most important to my child?

1

2

3

(Your answers may change as you work through the information and visit the schools.)

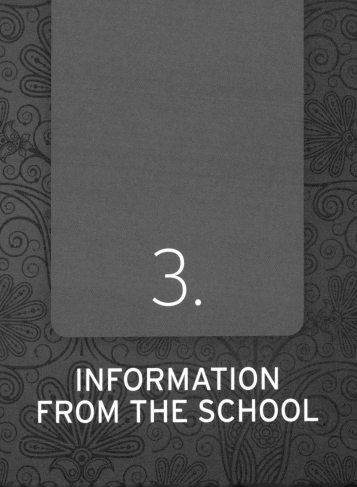

3.

INFORMATION
FROM THE SCHOOL

3. INFORMATION FROM THE SCHOOL

This information will probably come to you in the form of **brochures/prospectuses and websites**.

You will want to compare what they say and have some understanding of what this means.

They both contain factual information that it's worth comparing. In particular, look at:

THE VISION OR MISSION

THE SIZE

THE STRUCTURE OF THE DAY

THE WAY THE SCHOOL IS ORGANISED

THE CURRICULUM

But remember that **how** this information is presented is also important. So:

• Compare schools, not school brochures.

The job of the school brochure is to sell the school. The information shared and views expressed are intended to persuade you to choose that school and to conform to its expectations if it is popular.

- Consider what public face it shows.

What a school includes can tell you something about what it values and the opposite is also true.

- **How are students included?**

- **Are they smartly dressed?**

- **Do they look happy or proud?**

- **Are they engaged in activity?**

- **Can you see positive relationships?**

Look for comments from students and adults, not just quotations from OFSTED reports punctuated by words from the head.

- Remember school websites.

We don't yet associate public services with the net as readily as we do shopping or researching other types of information. (In some parts of the country, only a few people make secondary school applications on-line – this is not an area where we are very computer literate yet.)

Of course it should be relatively easy to keep a website updated. And if it isn't, an important question to ask on your visit is why not. A website is an important channel of two-way communication and a learning platform. It is not just a public relations tool.

THE VISION OR MISSION

This will be on the first page and should tell you clearly how the school sees itself and what it's trying to achieve, what it stands for and won't stand for. Vague statements about excellence and opportunity should be questioned during the visit.

Look at the pictures and images: they can tell you about priorities.

- The school building to show you tradition or state of the art new build?

- The Headteacher to show you authority and hierarchy?

- Students doing extra-curricular activities to show you a rounded education?

- New building plans to show you expansion and success?

- Students with or without the Head to show relationships?

Then add these to the type of **language** being used, as together they can reveal the type of community the school builds.

- Attainment
- Behaviour
- Consistency
- Discipline
- Lateness
- Routines
- Uniform

We associate these words with schools who see good behaviour as an end in itself (often because they have trouble securing it). Schools at the beginning of an improvement process from a low base may also choose these.

- Achievement
- Ambassadors
- Community
- Enthusiasm
- Happiness
- Learning
- Potential
- Relationships
- Responsibility
- Talents and qualities

These words we associate with schools who assume high standards of good behaviour but see that it flows from fair relationships, students feeling they belong and a sense of community. (This is just as true in a suburban girls' faith school as an inner city under-subscribed boys' school.)

Important to remember:

These are merely clues to a school's culture and cannot always be interpreted in the same way. Test out your assumptions by looking at results and OFSTED reports, as well as by visiting as many schools as you can. However, our experience has borne out the patterns described above.

(You may wish to add to these answers after your visits.)

What do we like about the school's mission or vision?

School 1

School 2

School 3

School 4

School 5

School 6

THE SIZE

· Schools vary greatly in size

Most have between 700 and 1,200 students but there are many smaller and much bigger.

A school with 700 and no Sixth Form will have 140 new students in year 7, probably in 5 classes (called Forms of Entry or FE).

An 11-16 school with 1,200 will have 240 new starters in year 7 probably with 8 FE.

· School success is not related to size

There is no substantial evidence that there is any link, so it will be the other factors related to size that matter to you.

What are the benefits?

BIG schools	SMALL schools
A wider range of subjects and courses	A community feel
Lots of extra curricular activities	A chance to shine and be known beyond your immediate form or year group
Anonymity if you want it	A more supportive environment
Good specialist facilities and teachers	Adults get to know students more quickly and needs and talents are spotted
High staff numbers so a good range of personalities and role models	
Lots of staff to share out the responsibilities of running the school	

BIG schools

Some large ones create a number of schools within the school to give the benefits of a smaller community with the funding and opportunities that size brings.

SMALL schools

Clever leaders in these places will compensate for the smaller budget and teaching staff by arranging the curriculum differently. You may see a carousel of subjects where students get to try things for a short period of time before moving on. You may see visitors delivering short drama or arts projects.

You may even see the university model of small tutorial groups and bigger lectures.

Remember, small independent schools have survived for years by being innovative in how they arrange their classes and curriculum.

The size of the Sixth Form

To be cost effective, a stand alone Sixth Form (not a collaborative offered with neighbouring schools or colleges) should have at least 200 students. Any less than that then either:

Key stages 3 and 4 will have to cost less to make Sixth Form teaching possible. This could mean big classes for children in Year 7 or less variety.

Or, there will be a narrow range of courses offered in the Sixth Form often with changes made at the last minute.

What does the school have in place to help my child's transition from a small school, where they are known by everyone, to a larger one?

School 1

School 2

School 3

School 4

School 5

School 6

THE STRUCTURE OF THE DAY

Start and finish times

There is a range, so consider:

- your child's patterns and preferences

- distance and time for travel to and from school

- your own work/life patterns (don't advertise this one - schools resent being seen as childminders).

Eating and playing times

When you visit, it will be important to look at eating spaces but in the meantime consider where there are breaks in the day with opportunities to snack and socialise. Some schools reduce them to minimise the need to provide supervision or extra curricular activities and so cause less inconvenience for adults.

Many schools will offer an early morning space or breakfast club where children can eat and finish homework, read newspapers or play board games and have contact with adults and other students.

After school activities

For your child: including the traditional clubs and activities like sport, music and drama. **Beware of schools that have none**. It's never a good sign and usually hints that the school is not well led.

For the wider community: (including yourself). They may include sport, adult and community learning , health, or council services such as libraries. . You will often hear of these referred to as extended services, and schools where many of these are available as extended schools.

What additional services or activities at the school might I/we use?

School 1

School 2

School 3

School 4

School 5

School 6

THE WAY THE SCHOOL IS ORGANISED

Horizontal year groups

- The traditional way: groups of children the same age, looked after by form tutors who track their attendance and academic progress as well as looking out for social development.

- A Head of Year runs the team and reports to a Deputy Head. They are keen on involving the children in making the form group the best at attendance, progress, raising money for charity, representing the school in sport and music etc.

- Teaching assistants and other adults may be attached to year groups or classes to reduce the student/teacher ratio.

Form groups may be arranged into Houses to allow students of different ages to engage in activities together, social or competitive and to feel part of a longer school tradition.

Vertical year groups

- Tutor groups across the age range: this is usually where a school wants to focus on the benefits of the more life-like experience of social mixing or to make a large school more friendly.

- It may be done to encourage role modelling and mentoring of older students with younger.

- It may also extend to actual learning, with students of similar ability, not age, working together in class.

Again, both approaches can bring success, so the key questions to ask are:

- Why has the school arranged things this way?

- Do the reasons appeal to you?

And absolutely key:

- Does it work? Ask the students. Guides during visits are great sources of unguarded truths, as is the casual question in a classroom where students are working.

Important to remember:

As with any question you ask, listen out for better opportunities for students, not greater convenience for adults.

A perfect example here is the length of the school lunch time. In some schools the lunch hour is reduced to minimise misbehaviour and to do away with the necessity for supervision.

Another school might reduce the lunch-time to shorten the day so that students can participate in a good range of after school activities.

The same decision builds different communities because it is made for different reasons.

(Yet another school will deal with the misbehaviour and supervision issues by lengthening the lunch-time, arranging activities that engage and interest the students and deploying adults across the whole of the school day rather that insisting that all staff have the same lunch time.)

Do the structure and organisation of the school suit us?

School 1

School 2

School 3

School 4

School 5

School 6

THE CURRICULUM

This is the heart of school life for your child and is made up of a number of elements that include the subjects offered.

In its totality, it should develop the knowledge and skills and attitudes that will prepare your child to succeed in a complex world.

And don't just look at outcomes, i.e exam results. These can belie the breadth of experiences the school offers your child.

Important to remember:

Look for messages of high aspiration and expectation at every turn. Make this your bottom line. Whatever your child's ability or interests, the curriculum and the adults who deliver it should inspire and motivate her/him to feel that s/he can be successful and make a difference in the world.

When you are talking to teachers, look for evidence of high expectations. Students need outstanding teaching to get them the highest grades.

Consider all these elements of the jigsaw:

Subjects

Extension work

Special needs

Enrichment (extra-curricular activities)

E learning (in school and at home)

Reporting progress

Information, advice and guidance (IAG)

Subjects

Government policy dictates the subjects taught and their content and these are reviewed and amended frequently. **www.capitaltalent.co.uk** for a current list of **national curriculum subjects**. In addition, expect to see:

- Learning building on key stages 1 and 2.

- An emphasis on numeracy, literacy and ICT.

- Opportunities for your child to discuss and reflect on major ideas and challenges for individuals and society, including: healthy lifestyles, safety, enterprise, environmental development, identity and cultural diversity, community participation, technology and the media.

Subject content includes an emphasis on skills. Expect to see,

- **Learning skills** - like self motivation and determination

- **Personal skills** - like team work and leadership

- **Emotional skills** - like resilience and respect

- **Thinking skills** - like synthesis and evaluation.

Whatever your child's strengths you will expect to see a pathway that suits his/her hopes for the future.

For some this will be a traditionally academic route that leads to A levels or the International Baccalaureate and then University.

For or others it will involve studying for a particular profession like engineering or information technology. For others again it may lead either to a work apprenticeship or qualifications that prepare for the world of work.

How well do the schools you are considering offer the pathways you want?

(You may want to add to these answers after your visits.)

School 1

School 2

School 3

School 4

School 5

School 6

Extension

This refers to ways the school supports students with particular strengths and talents.

Students could be given opportunities to progress at a faster rate than others or to take additional subjects.

Look for:

- Opportunities for early exam entry through additional classes or condensed courses.

- Subjects offering associated courses like statistics or an additional foreign language.

- After school lessons in unusual or creative areas; astronomy, politics, philosophy, Mandarin.

- An Exceptional Students register which includes individuals identified as having a particular strength or talent or a special need . There should be a clear outline of what provision is made for these students.

- Clubs that prepare students for universities like Oxford and Cambridge.

- A strong tradition of teaching to A* and A which should be present in every school even if in small numbers.

- A school policy that underpins the above, making clear that all students will be actively encouraged to progress at the fastest rate they can through their learning.

Important to remember

Some schools will give early entry to your child but will not give a later chance to improve the grade. This is relevant where your child will later choose a study path that demands an A or A*.

Special needs

By this we mean anything that may make access to learning in the curriculum a barrier; physical disability, emotional need, English as a new language, a medical condition, a fear or phobia, falling behind with numeracy or literacy.

(Some schools address the needs of these students along with the needs of the very able or talented and call them 'exceptional students.')

Acute need will only affect a few students and may result in a Statement of Special Educational Need but the principles are the same.

Good practice will include;

- Early and clearly communicated ways of identifying need

- A broad definition

- Most special needs being met through an annual review of the curriculum

- Most support happening within a larger group

- Short bursts of highly focused intervention

- 1 - 1 support or mentoring

- Some mixing of students of different ages

- Creative use of adults like teaching assistants, youth workers, learning mentors

- A clear focus on numeracy and literacy skills

- Learning groups to address specific needs like girls only science or course work support.

Enrichment (Extra-curricular activities)

Enrichment is a term used by schools to describe those activities, opportunities and experiences that happen outside lessons even if they are linked to particular subjects.

They include anything from learning to juggle to international exchanges.

Some schools see these as so central to learning and growing up that they have a minimum entitlement that every child has access to.

It will include the things that you should expect to see in all the schools you visit.

- Lunchtime activities like board games or sport, business and enterprise clubs, debating teams

- Cultural opportunities like visits to the theatre and opera

- Trips including some abroad

- Choir, band or opportunities to play an instrument

- Performance opportunities in drama, dance and music

- Contributions to the community like voluntary service

- Structured courses that develop other skills like sports leader awards or the Duke of Edinburgh scheme.

And you may see unusual offers to engage students broadly. We've seen things as wide ranging and interesting as circus skills, Go Kart racing (and making), martial arts, dance classes and golf.

Basically, if a school makes use of all the adults' interests (perhaps involving parents too), it results in a great mix and shows students the extra dimension a passionate interest or just a relaxing hobby can add to life.

The focus here is on participation and commitment, not excellence.

E learning

Information technology is part of every subject. At some point schools should offer opportunities for students to;

- Use interactive whiteboards for learning

- Use the net and word process

- Learn all the basic IT software tools

- Complete whole courses on line

- Take assessments on line

- Use a Virtual Learning Environment to store their work and access resources

- Collaborate with students elsewhere on line.

Although schools have developed these to varying degrees, a school with very little, disadvantages your child.

Reporting progress

When does the school report to you on progress?

- You want an update early in year 7 to know that your child is settling in. This might be a general comment rather that specific detail on what has been learned, but it is intended to reassure you and iron out any early issues.

- Children don't improve because they are measured but assessment is necessary for the teachers to know where attitudes, skills and knowledge still need to be developed. With this in mind, expect frequent assessment of progress that falls between 6 weeks and 1 term. Any less frequently and the teacher's response to your child's needs is too slow.

How does the school report to you?

- Reporting that includes you and your child in setting targets as part of the process encourages independence and respects your influence as a parent.

- Some schools will have a Virtual Learning Environment (a VLE) or a Managed Learning Environment (MLE). This allows them to communicate with you and your child easily and frequently using the internet about:

- Lesson content

- Homework

- Your child's attendance

- Your child's effort and attitude to learning

- Progress

- Your child will also be able to store work there that can be accessed by you or them from anywhere over the internet.

- Of course, if you don't have access or are not very comfortable using ICT, you might prefer traditional communication.

Information, Advice and Guidance (IAG)

This area includes advice to your child on subject choices, exam entries and study and career paths.

 For the current list of what the school must provide under **Information Advice and Guidance (IAG)** go to **www.capitaltalent.co.uk**.

Important to remember:

Look at this curriculum offer as a whole and consider whether there are enough opportunities here for your child to become the kind of person s/he aspires to be and you would hope for. You are looking for fun, challenge and personal development as well as success.

Remember the things that have stayed in your mind all these years after leaving school:

- probably not hot afternoons listening to one more teacher read something from one more text book;

- more likely the first time you stepped into the spotlight and onto the stage or abseiling down a cliff face in the rain.

- These things aren't always obvious on the limetable or measured by the information in our next section, but we all know how formative and vital they are.

What free enrichment and extension activities will my child have access to?

School 1

School 2

School 3

School 4

School 5

School 6

What other questions do I want to ask each school about the curriculum?

School 1

School 2

School 3

School 4

School 5

School 6

What pathways does each school offer in the Sixth Form and how do they compare to other local offers?

(Further Education Colleges, Sixth Form Colleges, schools with large or long-established Sixth Forms.)

Level 1 = Work-related
Level 2 = Vocational
Level 3 = A level equivalent

School 1

Level 1

Level 2

Level 3

School 2

Level 1

Level 2

Level 3

School 3

Level 1

Level 2

Level 3

School 4

Level 1

Level 2

Level 3

School 5

Level 1

Level 2

Level 3

School 6

Level 1

Level 2

Level 3

4.

INFORMATION
ABOUT THE SCHOOL

4. INFORMATION ABOUT THE SCHOOL

In this section we concentrate on what you can learn from:

EXAM RESULTS

OFSTED

EXAM RESULTS

We live in a time of targets and data. There are many types of data produced by and about schools and they are a rich source of comparison.

But don't forget the adage, 'lies, damn lies and statistics.' Exam results can be the school equivalent. Each piece of statistical information must be seen as part of the whole picture. Obviously schools will emphasise those pieces which show their school in the best light so it will be up to you to research the full story.

You need to have the answers to the following questions. We tell you how to answer them, why they are important and where to go for more information.

Does this school get good **GCSE RESULTS**?

Do the students in this school make good **PROGRESS**?

Do **ALL STUDENTS MAKE PROGRESS**?

Do all the **SUBJECTS** do well?

Are there opportunities for students to achieve the **HIGHEST GRADES**?

Go to **www.capitaltalent.co.uk** for **school results** for each school.

 Go to **www.capitaltalent.co.uk** for more information on **understanding exam results** including up to date information on national averages and trends.

GCSE results

GCSE results are reported and recorded as the percentage of students in each school who achieve 5 or more good GCSEs including English and Maths.

- Good is defined as a C grade or above. (Remember, pass grades go from A* to G).

- **The magic number** you are looking for is something above 50% as this is in line with national averages.

A. Are results at (or about at) the national average?

The very lowest acceptable benchmark for the government is 30% as this percentage often equates to other indicators of success across the school. However, there are many, many examples of good schools who achieve less than 50% for very good reasons, some of which will become clear as you read below.

B. Are results going up year after year?

Look at the last 3 or 4 years and look for an upward trend. (Don't worry if there are slight fluctuations year on year, each year of students is different.) Obviously if the school already achieves 99 or 100 % GCSEs then it's not possible to improve forever on this figure. This is where the information below can help you to compare schools.

- The percentage of students who achieve 5 or more good GCSEs **without English and Maths** is also calculated, so be careful that you are not presented with this figure as the key percentage: it is not the one used for national comparison.

- Do compare the two scores. A big difference suggests that the school is using vocational qualifications equivalent to 2 or 4 GCSEs at A*-C to boost examination results and not concentrating on basic academic skills.

- This GCSE figure alone will not tell you enough about what experience your child will have of school. You need to see it alongside the overall curriculum offer explained in Section 3 and the progress measure explained next.

Progress

Progress' or Value Added (VA) is the measure of how much students learn during their 5 years in secondary school. It takes a benchmark from their arrival in year seven and then uses GCSE results to see how each far child has travelled. It allows you to compare schools and should be looked at with the GCSE results.

- **The magic number** you are looking for in a school is 1000 or more. Each year this is re-calculated as the benchmark so anything above 1000 is above the national average and anything below 1000 is below the national average.

- A word of warning about this figure: you need to see how many of the children who take exams in year 11 have been in the school since year 7. **This is called coverage and is expressed as a percentage**. Schools with very high turnover of students or empty places which are filled during the school year may have a figure below 50%. This makes the VA meaningless.

- OFSTED inspectors use progress measures just as much as GCSE results when making their judgements in an inspection and they look to make sure that **all** students make progress not just those in particular ability, ethnic or social groups.

- For parents and carers comparing schools it is a vital piece of information. It can tell you which of two schools with similar GCSE results makes more progress with their students.

- It can tell you whether a school with less than 50% GCSEs makes better progress with students than a school with GCSEs way above 50%.

All students make progress

To decide whether **all students make progress** or just particular groups, look at the measure called Contextual Value Added (CVA). It is like Value Added but tries to take account of some of the things outside a school's control: gender, family circumstances, special educational needs, movement between schools, ethnicity, the results students achieved at primary school.

- It is worked out in a similar way to Value Added and again the **magic number** is 1000.

Subjects

Subjects are compared within schools using a measure called Average Points Score (APS).

- If your child already has particular interests and strengths this number will help you to see whether relevant subjects in the school are strong. If your child is considering medicine you want a strong science department. If your child is considering a career in the leisure industry, you want a strong PE department.

Highest grades

Look at the percentage of A*s and As achieved in the school to see that students reach the **highest grades**.

This is a good indication of whether the school has outstanding teaching and outstanding teaching supports children in fulfilling their potential at every level and in every subject.

School

School 1

School 2

School 3

School 4

School 5

School 6

Beware of any suggestions that the school has no students who can achieve these grades.

- The national average of A* grades is running at around the mid teens depending on where you are in the country.

- Look across the curriculum to see that every subject achieves the highest grades.

Are results at or about at the national average?	Are results going up over a 3 year period?	Are the progress measures good?	What percentage of the students get A*s and As

Important to remember:

Only a small percentage of children get straight A*s at GCSE: the system is designed to share out the grades.

Still, you want your child to do the best s/he can and the school to do its best by them.

You want to know that the school can walk the line between encouraging every child to reach for the stars and accepting that for most children this will not mean straight As.

OFSTED

OFSTED, the Office for Standards in Education, Children's Services and Skills, monitors and regulates the quality of education in Secondary schools. It uses a Framework underpinned by law and is overseen by the Her Majesty's Chief Inspector.

The Framework obviously changes in response to government priorities and to new understandings of what will improve education for our children but it remains one of the most useful and accurate ways to compare schools because of the quality and experience of the colleagues carrying out inspections and the rigour of their training.

Using a Report

At the beginning of any report you will see **a description of the school**, contextual information that is not judged.

Then the key for inspection grades:

Grade 1 Outstanding

Grade 2 Good

Grade 3 Satisfactory

Grade 4 Inadequate

The report is then broken down into a number of sections that include one of these inspection grades and a description of the main things the inspectors found.

 Go to **www.capitaltalent.co.uk** for a link to all **OFSTED reports**.

In the following table we have summarised these sections, a description of their main content and some useful comments.

Report Sections	Description
Overall effectiveness of the school	This grade is an amalgamation of all the other evidence and grades and is the grade that is most often reported in association with the school.

This section also includes a statement about the school's **capacity to improve**.

If the school has a sixth form or any early years provision, you will see a comment and judgement here.

At the end of this section you will see the list of things the school must concentrate on to improve. |
| **Achievement and standards** | This will tell you about the exam results and how they compare both nationally and to comparable schools.

It will also tell you about the achievements of particular groups. |

Comments

Capacity to improve is very important because it tells you how likely it is that the school will continue to improve over the years of your child's education there. Look for a statement that includes the words 'good' or 'outstanding.'

The list of improvements should be neither long nor basic.

Look here to see that students of whatever background and ability do well right across the subjects.

Report Sections	Description
Personal development and well-being	This section considers attendance, exclusions, to what extent the school is a community and how well the school meets students cultural, moral and spiritual needs.
Quality of provision This section covers 3 areas;	
· Teaching and learning	How well lessons are taught.
· Curriculum and other activities	What subjects are taught.
· Care, guidance and support	How the staff take care of your children, monitor their progress and advise them on their futures.
Leadership and management	This includes the leadership of Headteacher, governors and anyone else in the school with a leadership role.

Comments

This section can tell you a lot about how happy your child will be at school and what opportunities will be available beyond the timetabled subjects.

Satisfactory teaching is not a good sign.

The focus is on whether the subjects are appropriate for the students there at any given time.

This is the key 'happiness' measure.

This measure is vital. Again, this is an area where 'satisfactory' is not good enough even if a Head is new. It is better to have a 'good' Head in a satisfactory school than a 'satisfactory' Head in a 'good' school.

At the end of the report you will see some tables with additional grades. These are the separate judgments in each of the above sections that add up to the overall grades. They are useful to see if particular elements are of interest or concern for you.

Important to remember:

OFSTED inspectors have an amazing collective experience of comparing schools so they know how to spot a good school.

OFSTED do get it wrong sometimes. A lead inspector occasionally lets personal pre-occupation determine which judgements hold the most weight and this can sway the overall balance.

The school will have changed a lot since the last Inspection. That might be 3 or 5 years ago. Check the date on the last report.

A school may be very different within 12 months of a new Head starting. Check the name of the Headteacher on the last report.

The parent/carer questionnaire used as part of the Inspection is a measure of how well the school involves parents. Low numbers can be a sign of remote Headteachers or/and unsupportive parents.

The OFSTED site will allow you to get an overview of all the schools in your local area.

Go to **www.capitaltalent.co.uk** for more **information on OFSTED** including:

- who carries out inspections, how often and why

- useful tips on using the OFSTED site

- the link for downloading school reports

- a chart of common terminology inspectors use in reports

- some tips on what inspectors say and what it really means

- what it means if a school's overall grade is 4 (inadequate)

- which judgements in the report MUST be above a 4.

Use the last OFSTED reports from each school
to complete the questions in the chart.

School	When was the school's last OFSTED and who was the Head?
School 1	
School 2	
School 3	
School 4	
School 5	
School 6	

What is the school's overall OFSTED judgement for the last inspection?	What was the teaching and learning grade?	What was the leadership and management grade?	What was the care, guidance and support grade?

5.

THE VISIT

5. THE VISIT

And so, the moment of truth. Does your visit support what you have learned so far about the school or does it contradict it?

Here we summarise the main things the trained eye looks for and give you some questions to ask.

You are likely to be looking for a number of things at any one time but for ease of reading we have divided the section into:

THE LEARNING ENVIRONMENT IN ACTION

THE HEADTEACHER

THE RELATIONSHIPS

THE LEARNING ENVIRONMENT IN ACTION

Reception

You will probably arrive in reception where you will start forming impressions immediately. Just like meeting someone for the first time, these first few seconds are vital. Record what you think and consider whether or not what you subsequently see backs up your first impressions.

- Don't be put off by dilapidated buildings with leaking ceilings and draughty windows or seduced by pristine new premises. They are rarely linked to the quality of education.

- Of course, it's better to be in an uplifting building than a depressing one but that comes from how you use what you've got. So look for how much care is taken of what is there.

- Many schools will have an adult only or limited student access reception. This is the public face of the school so expect it to be welcoming and clean. There should be useful public information and evidence of student work, opportunity and success.

- Look at dates on information and display: they should be current.

If a school can't get this right, what hope is there for the rest of the environment where hundreds of adults and children work and learn every day?

Learning areas

Once you are past the reception think about how the space will feel to an 11 year old. Are there attempts to make it welcoming and friendly with the use of furniture, colour or pictures?

- Look for a variety of teaching styles.

Expect to see that:

- the lay-out of furniture in the classrooms or learning spaces shows flexibility

- the teacher's desk is not always at the front or even visible to you.

(If you want a more traditional learning environment look for desks facing forward to the teacher.)

Look for evidence that the walls (and the ceilings) are used for learning. One third of children will learn more from these than anything they hear. Look for:

- key words

- definitions and formulae

- good work displayed to motivate

- exemplars so students know how to get it right at different grades

- rewards given or awards won

- an interactive whiteboard.

Look for evidence that your child is encouraged to work independently and so grow in confidence and self-discipline. Some examples include:

- tables arranged so that 4 or 6 students can sit and work together

- the marking criteria that the teacher uses on display so that students can learn for themselves what it is they need to do to improve and progress

- displayed work (or in any exercise books you have the chance to see), to have some self assessment or suggestions from fellow students on how to improve.

Look for evidence of good leadership. Within departments look for:

- tidy and well presented rooms

- a team approach to display

- some evidence of what department you are in

- resources and books well kept and organised.

These can say something about how the Head of that subject sees their role and how individual teachers and adults feel about their work.

The public spaces are the responsibility of the Leadership Team of the school and tell you about their standards and priorities.

Expect to have access to all teaching areas, not just the well equipped and interesting ones.

Social spaces

These should be student focused with some balance between the academic and the social. They will tell you something about the kind of culture or community the school is building. A good combination will include:

- places to sit and talk

- places to read and play quiet games

- places to run around

- places to be on a cold or rainy day (some schools lock the students out of the building or parts of it at break times and lunch times)

- library and IT use during free time

- separate spaces for year 7s to help settle them in

- organised and structured activities, clubs and societies.

Look at nooks and crannies. A school can't help how it's designed but you are looking for signs that these are safe spaces, well lit with display, pictures or soft seating for privacy. You don't want to see signs of neglect, graffiti, litter, or defaced display.

It's quite common to see observation cameras in parts of schools now in common with the move to put them in other public spaces. They can be invaluable for ensuring your child's safety but do not expect to see them predominate. Safe relationships make safe schools.

Many schools have student lockers for storage. These need to be well-maintained and located in a safe and secure place. Many schools put them on well-used corridors and have a different area for each year group.

The toilets and the dining hall

We want to emphasise the importance of these two areas for young people. When they are wrong, they are constantly and repeatedly cited by students as the main causes of anxiety at school. And again you will learn a lot about the culture of the school and the predominant relationships from what you see.

In the dining hall ask about or look for:

- the way students come in to and go out of the dining hall

- a safe space to wait

- a warm space to wait

- a rota for eating

- a welcoming and inviting eating area

- proper metal cutlery and ceramic plates

- clear information about menus and prices.

In the toilets ask about or look for:

- toilet paper

- easy access (not locked outer doors)

- privacy.

Some clever Heads have built toilets in single units directly off well-used corridors. This removes all the problems associated with large groups of young people going in to toilets at the same time.

Important to remember:

Some schools operate daytime as well as evening visits. Obviously daytime visits do not suit the working patterns of most of us but if you get the opportunity to see the school in action, welcome it with open arms.

Many schools will agree to visits during the day even if they don't do organised tours. Seeing the school in action allows you to test the truth of their marketing and to experience relationships in action.

Even if you can't get there during the day, do what OFSTED inspectors do, stand near the entrance as children are arriving in the morning or leaving in the afternoon. You will see a lot about relationships and safety at these times.

In busy urban areas you may see the growing trend of adults using students in fluorescent jackets to help smaller children across busy roads or use shops.

You may also see police on bikes, in cars or on horses. Don't be alarmed by this. It's a normal part of community policing and part of the trend to integrate services.

What was welcoming about each school environment?

School 1

School 2

School 3

School 4

School 5

School 6

What did we see that suggested that there would be a variety of teaching styles?

School 1

School 2

School 3

School 4

School 5

School 6

THE HEADTEACHER

At some point during your visit the Head will address you.

Style

- What approach does the Head take to the audience? Do you feel patronised or invited to partnership? Do you feel welcomed or privileged?

- Do you feel inspired? This isn't all there is to Headship and not all Heads need to look or sound the same but the Head must have presence and inspire confidence.

- But beware of Headteachers indulging in spin. Running a school is a sophisticated business.

- Trust your instincts.

Content

In the address, does the Head focus on what won't be tolerated?

- In a traditional, successful oversubscribed school the Head may talk about what's expected of you and your child: exam results, uniform, standards you must uphold.

- In a challenging school there may be comparable messages about behaviour or attendance.

- Both may be related more to the school's reputation than to your child's education.

Both may reflect an organisation that focuses more on being well-run and organised than your child's individual needs.

Or does the Head focus on:

- what the children achieve and obstacles they overcome

- opportunities afforded them and taken

- competitions they won, trips they went on, how the school improves their chances

- how they are involved in the community and develop themselves as young people?

And are messages about OFSTED reports or exam results delivered in the spirit of celebration and success or do they seem like the whole story?

You may be addressed by students. A school keen on participation may see this as an opportunity for a student to gain valuable public speaking practice. A school keen on excellence will present a confident student with something clear and structured to say.

Important to remember:

A small but growing number of schools are run by Executive Headteachers, colleagues who have been very successful in one or more previous Headships and are invited to co-ordinate the work of 2 or more schools. In some cases the schools federate under one governing body.

If this Executive Headteacher addresses you on a school visit, bear in mind that your subsequent contact with the school will probably be through a Head of school who will be responsible for its day to day running.

THE RELATIONSHIPS

In this key area you want to look at the different relationships within the school. They will tell you something about the culture in which your child will be learning and socialising.

Consider whether the relationships are based on hierarchy and positional power or are they based on equality and ability. One builds a more traditional and structured type of environment, the other might encourage expression, independence and confidence.

You have to decide which you prefer. If you build one thing at home but send your child to a school environment that expects the other, you are asking for conflict.

Of course the ideal is a middle way where children learn how to behave appropriately according to each context.

Student relationships

- Look for and listen to how students treat each other.

- Are there messages about respect for difference, belongings, safety?

- Do students seem happy?

- Do you see students working together in mixed age, gender and ethnicity groups?

- How do students talk to each other?

- Look and listen for structured solutions for dealing with conflict that include peer mentoring and support, mediation, conflict resolution.

- Look and listen for clear messages about how the school deals with and prepares students to deal with bullying. There should not only be a policy but practical advice that's known by all.

Adult/student relationships

- Look at and listen to how the teachers talk to the students around them and don't assume that every teacher talks to young people the way they talk to you as an adult.

- Students in attitude surveys ask that the adults who work with them be fair, firm and fun.

- Look at and listen to how students respond when you approach. This tells you to what extent the presence of adults encourages the students to modify and reflect on their own behaviour. This is one of those important things that doesn't always go hand-in-hand with good exam results.

- Look and listen for language that focuses on what the school wants students to do rather than what it doesn't want them to do. 'Walk in corridors' works many more times than 'don't run in corridors' and creates a more positive culture.

- Take the opportunity to talk to students.

Put the following questions in your own words. They build a really clear picture if you use them several times in each school and then compare them.

- **What are your favourite three places in the school and why?**

- **What is your least favourite place in the school and why?**

- **Why did you chose the school and has it lived up to your expectations?**

- **What would you change about the school if you could?** (This should show you a clearly communicated vision that involves the students.)

- **What are the main plans or priorities for the school at the moment?** (This should show you a sense of community.)

- **What is your ambition or what do you want to do at 16?**
(This should show you high expectations and good IAG.)

- **Do you have a student council and what changes has it brought about?** (This should show real student influence on how the school is run.)

 www.capitaltalent.co.uk if you want a **student questionnaire**.

Important to remember:

While you are making your assessment of the school during your visit, the school will be making its assessment of you. If you are keen to be considered, dress and act in a way that is appropriate to that setting.

Ensure that any children who accompany you do the same.

And think of what message you are sending if you stop your tour to answer your mobile phone, talk across your student guide or arrive late at any performances or addresses.

What did we see and hear that suggested that the school has high aspirations and expectations?

School 1

School 2

School 3

School 4

School 5

School 6

6.

PLAYING YOUR PART

6. **PLAYING YOUR PART**

Your child will learn best if you and the school work in partnership. Look for clues about your ongoing relationship and clarity about your role and theirs. Bear in mind:

- School and home need to work together: you will want a school that complements your home life and your values so that your child doesn't come into conflict with you or the school.

- Schools are social not private places: the school will want you to understand that while your child is an individual, individualism (the frequent need to be an exception to rules and routines) doesn't help the community or your child cope with real life. The school will have a particular ethos and rightly expect your child to respect and contribute to this.

And so consider,

How are you dealt with if you approach the school?

By staff in reception in person or on the telephone?

- Promptly, courteously and helpfully?
  Or as if you are interrupting something and a nuisance?

How are you referred to on the website or in literature?

- Look for evidence of 'partnership.'

What opportunities are there for your involvement?

- Joint teacher/student/parent target setting through academic review.

- A traditional PTA for fundraising and social opportunities.

- The chance to stand for election to be a parent governor for decision making opportunities.

- Reading, literacy, numeracy or mentoring schemes to help students directly.

- Special events for dads or mums, including family learning.

How and when does the school communicate with you?

- Your child's progress and learning through a VLE/MLE or email.

- Text messaging.

- Open evenings/days to view work, performances, successes.

- Regular newsletters.

When and how are your suggestions and opinions sought?

- Annual attitude surveys.

- Headteacher surgeries.

- An on-line parent forum.

Often schools will have a home - school agreement which you are asked to read and sign on arrival in year 7. It will list the school rules, times of the day, what to do in the case of absence, school uniform and so on. Good ones will include what your child can expect from the school in terms of fair treatment and curriculum entitlement and outline its principles and values.

What did we see and hear that suggested we would have an effective relationship with the school?

School 1

School 2

School 3

School 4

School 5

School 6

FINALLY

You have reached the end of this thorough preparation to make one of your most far-reaching decisions as a parent or carer. The comparison chart included in your tin allows you to summarise your key thoughts from each section of the guide.

Use what you have written here to complete the columns on the chart. It is not repetition but a summary that allows you to make a judgement about each of the key things. Try not to take short cuts now in transferring what you have found to the charts. As you go through your guide, you will be amazed at how much you forget from each school once you move on to looking at the next one.

We wish you every success in getting your preferred choices. Whatever your emotions have told you during the visits, go back to your research, your needs and ambitions and take everything into account before making your choices.

Good luck. Please email us with any feedback you have about the guide and we'd like to hear from you next March to know if you got your first, second or third choice, email us at **feedback@ capitaltalent.co.uk**. We believe that informed parents making informed choices will improve the system.